Jesus Feed the Hungry

"They don't need to go away.
You give them something to eat."
—Matthew 14:16

ZONDERKIDZ

The Beginner's Bible Jesus Feeds the Hungry

Copyright © 2012 by Zondervan
Illustrations © 2012 by Zondervan

Requests for information should be addressed to:

Zonderkidz, 5300 Patterson Ave SE, Grand Rapids, Michigan 49530

Library of Congress Cataloging-in-Publication Data

Jesus feeds the hungry.
    p.   cm. — (The beginner's bible)
    ISBN 978-0-310-72519-0 (pbk.)
    1. Feeding of the five thousand (Miracle)—Juvenile literature. I. Zonderkidz.
BT367.F4J472   2012
232.9'55—dc23

2012018376

Written by: Crystal Bowman
Editor: Mary Hassinger
Cover & Interior Design: Cindy Davis

Printed in China

ZONDERVAN.com/
AUTHORTRACKER
follow your favorite authors

8 19 20 21 22 23 /LPC/ 12 11 10 9 8 7 6 5 4 3

Many people followed Jesus wherever he went.
Some of the people wanted Jesus to heal them.
Some wanted to ask him questions. Others just
wanted to listen to his stories. Jesus loved the
people very much. But sometimes Jesus was tired,
and he wanted to be alone in a quiet place, where
he could rest.

One day, Jesus got into a boat with Philip, Andrew, John, and his other disciples. They went across the lake so they could get away from the crowd for a while and rest. But they couldn't get away. The people ran along the shore to the place where Jesus was going. They ran so fast they got there before Jesus did.

When the boat reached the shore, the people were waiting for Jesus. Jesus climbed out of the boat and walked toward the people.

He looked at the big crowd and felt sorry for them. He knew they had come especially to see him, so he did not want to send them away. Jesus spent time with the people. He placed his hands on the sick people and healed them.

Jesus talked to the people and taught them many things. He told them that God loved them. He told them to be kind to others. He told them to obey God and to do what was right. The people stayed and listened to Jesus for a long, long time.

Soon the sun was going down, and it was getting late in the day.

The disciples were worried. They said to Jesus, "It's already late, and there is nothing to eat around here. Send the people to the nearby towns so they can find food to eat and places to sleep."

But Jesus said to Philip, "Don't send them away. We need to feed them. Where can we buy bread so we will have enough food to feed all these people?" Jesus said this to see what Philip would say. He already knew what he was going to do.

Philip shook his head and said, "We cannot feed this many people! We would have to work many months in order to earn enough money to buy food for them."

"How much food do we have right now?" asked Jesus.
"Go and find out."

Andrew found a boy who had some food. He brought the boy to Jesus.

"Here is a boy who will share his food with us," said Andrew. "But he only has five loaves of barley bread and two small fish. That is not enough to feed this big, hungry crowd."

Jesus said to his disciples, "Tell everyone to sit down on the grass. Have them sit in groups of about fifty people."

So that is what they did. All of the men, women, and children sat
down on the grass in groups. They waited to see what Jesus would do.

Jesus took a loaf of bread in his hands and looked up toward heaven. He thanked God for the bread and asked God to bless it. He broke the loaves of bread into pieces and gave the pieces to his disciples to give to the people.

Then Jesus took the fish in his hands and thanked God for the fish. He asked God to bless the fish, and he broke them into pieces—just like he did with the bread. Jesus gave the pieces of fish to his disciples so they could feed the people.

The disciples gave the bread and fish to the people. And to the disciples' surprise they never ran out of food! They had enough bread and fish to feed everyone. Over five thousand people ate until their stomachs were full. There was even food left over!

Jesus said to his disciples, "Pick up the pieces of fish and bread that are left over. Do not waste any of the food." So the disciples picked up all the pieces of bread and fish that had not been eaten, and they put the food into baskets. There was enough food left over to fill twelve large baskets!

When the people saw this miracle that Jesus had done, they knew he was not an ordinary man.

"He must be the Prophet we have been waiting for!" they said.

Jesus knew it was time for him to leave the people for a while.
So he went up into the hills where he could rest, be alone, and pray.